Dear Parent:
Your child's love of reading starts here!

Every child learns to read in a different way and at his or her own speed. Some go back and forth between reading levels and read favorite books again and again. Others read through each level in order. You can help your young reader improve and become more confident by encouraging his or her own interests and abilities. From books your child reads with you to the first books he or she reads alone, there are I Can Read Books for every stage of reading:

SHARED READING
Basic language, word repetition, and whimsical illustrations, ideal for sharing with your emergent reader

BEGINNING READING
Short sentences, familiar words, and simple concepts for children eager to read on their own

READING WITH HELP
Engaging stories, longer sentences, and language play for developing readers

READING ALONE
Complex plots, challenging vocabulary, and high-interest topics for the independent reader

ADVANCED READING
Short paragraphs, chapters, and exciting themes for the perfect bridge to chapter books

I Can Read Books have introduced children to the joy of reading since 1957. Featuring award-winning authors and illustrators and a fabulous cast of beloved characters, I Can Read Books set the standard for beginning readers.

A lifetime of discovery begins with the magical words **"I Can Read!"**

Visit www.icanread.com for information
on enriching your child's reading experience.

Ree Drummond and Diane deGroat gratefully
acknowledge the editorial and artistic contributions
of Amanda Glickman and Rick Whipple.

I Can Read Book® is a trademark of HarperCollins Publishers.

Charlie the Ranch Dog: Charlie's New Friend Text copyright © 2014 by Ree Drummond. Cover art copyright © 2014 Diane deGroat. Interior art copyright © 2014 by HarperCollins Publishers. All rights reserved. Manufactured in China. No part of this book may be used or reproduced in any manner whatsoever without written permission except in the case of brief quotations embodied in critical articles and reviews. For information address HarperCollins Children's Books, a division of HarperCollins Publishers, 10 East 53rd Street, New York, NY 10022

www.icanread.com

Library of Congress catalog card number: 2013943663
ISBN 978-0-06-221915-2 (trade bdg.) —ISBN 978-0-06-221914-5 (pbk.)
Typography by Victor Joseph Ochoa

13 14 15 16 17   SCP   10 9 8 7 6 5 4 3 2 1   ❖   First Edition

CHARLIE
the Ranch Dog
CHARLIE'S NEW FRIEND

based on the CHARLIE THE RANCH DOG books
by REE DRUMMOND, The Pioneer Woman
and DIANE deGROAT

HARPER
An Imprint of HarperCollinsPublishers

Bam! A bright light hits my face.

I cover my eyes with my floppy ears.

Oh. It's just the sun.

Wait. What?

The sun!

Yesterday was cold and rainy.

So was the day before.

I didn't get any ranch work done!

Today will be extra busy.

Sniff, sniff.

Where's my bacon breakfast?

I'd better find Mama.

I spot Mama in the garden.

The grass is warm on my paws.

Sniff, sniff. Flowers!

Wait. Is that a bird?

Squirrel! I chase him up a tree.

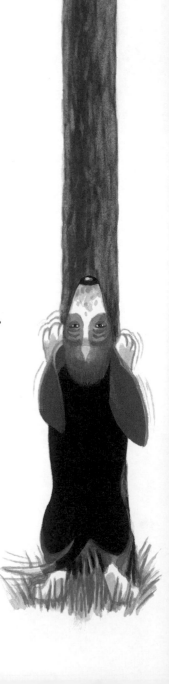

Wait. Wait! Is that a rabbit?

Chasing rabbits is the best!

Mama doesn't see the rabbit hopping.

She is digging up carrots.

But I know what Mr. Rabbit is up to.

RRRRRROOOWW-OOOOOH!

I howl and take a giant, running leap.

That rabbit is fast!

He grabs a carrot

and jumps right over my head.

Oh, I don't think so, Mr. Rabbit.

I'm the boss of this ranch.

No one steals from Mama

and gets away with it!

The chase is on.

Huff. Puff. Phew!

My short legs weren't made for this.

You can hop, but you can't hide!

Huh?

Where did Mr. Rabbit go?

Sniff, sniff.

Did Mr. Rabbit go down this hole?

When will he come out?

I guess I'll have to wait.

The sun feels so warm on my fur.
Maybe I'll lie down and rest,
just for one second.

Ouch!

Rabbit feet smack my back.

He's a hopping machine!

I'll never catch him.

Who invented chasing rabbits, anyway?

Chasing rabbits is the worst!

Why can't we just be friends?

Oh, right.

Because he's a carrot thief.

Grrr. My stomach rumbles.

I forgot to eat breakfast!

This is all Mr. Rabbit's fault.

I'm so hungry.

Wait. Hold on!

I have an idea.

No one is in the garden.

I sniff until I find a ripe carrot.

I dig it up with my front paws.

"Yoo-hoo, Mr. Rabbit.

Are you home?"

No answer.

I'll have to wait again.

Nap time!

Sniff, sniff!

My nose wakes me up.

Mr. Rabbit!

He can't escape down his hole.

I'm lying on top of it.

He looks around everywhere

and wiggles his pink nose.

Mr. Rabbit is shaking all over.

The carrot is in my mouth.

I stand and smile my biggest smile

so he won't be afraid.

I take one step forward and—ZOOM!

Mr. Rabbit is gone in a flash

back down his rabbit hole.

The next day, I guard the garden.

Mr. Rabbit stays away all morning.

At noon, I bring him a carrot lunch.

I don't wait this time.

After a yummy bacon dinner,

I head across the pasture.

There is no sign of the carrot.

Mr. Rabbit pokes his head up.
"If you stop taking carrots
without asking," I say,
"I will share them with you."

Mr. Rabbit offers me

a nibble of carrot.

Ugh! Yuck!

I'm so happy to be
a bacon-eating ranch dog
instead of a carrot-eating rabbit.